I Will Not Fold These Maps

لن أطوي هذه الخرائط

'Kareem's searing, irreverent poems, in the original Arabic and in Elkamel's translation, observe, criticize, distort. Both simple and complex, they challenge reality and authority. "You can't trust anyone who doesn't like oranges," she writes, and you want to nod in agreement. It was a pleasure to read this book: a serious and playful, intimate and political, surreal and familiar song.'
– Zeina Hashem Beck, author of *O* and *Louder than Hearts*

'Mona Kareem writes geographies of exile with teeth, and with a cutting whimsy, that constantly upturns the landscapes around and inside her. Her verse is a tilling of the heart.'
– Khairani Barokka, author of *Ultimatum Orangutan*

'Mona Kareem's poems wriggle against the constraints of borders and reductive cartographies. Hers is a ruthlessly generous poetry, one which burrows under the skin of various Gulf/s, exposing the subterranean and subjugated, the echoes of dying cities and resurrected histories. In these poems, exile is a purgatory, an interrupted horizon. The migrant and the poet share a body. Boundaries are obliterated and overthrown. Kareem inhabits this state of suspension, inviting us to do the same in our reading.'
– Momtaza Mehri, author of *Bad Diaspora Poems*

'Mona Kareem skips and leaps across her poems with the patience of one who believes in the power of silences, of blank spaces, that can liberate perception from the hyperreflex of easy identification.'
– Fady Joudah, author of *Tethered to Stars*

'Each poem retraces a memory in the making, its imagination marked by physical objects, trembling reality, characters who are exiled at home, and ghosts in exile. Beautifully translated by Sara Elkamel, Mona Kareem's poetic maps cannot be folded; her geography is one of adjustment, error, and erasure, and her voice is firmly engraved in each line.'
– Iman Mersal, author of *The Threshold*

Mona Kareem

I Will Not Fold These Maps
لن أطوي هذه الخرائط

Translated from Arabic by
Sara Elkamel

poetry
translation
centre

First published in 2023
by the Poetry Translation Centre Ltd
The Albany, Douglas Way, London, SE8 4AG

www.poetrytranslation.org

ISBN: 978-1-7398948-3-2

A catalogue record for this book is available from the British Library

Typeset in Minion / Adobe Arabic
by Poetry Translation Centre Ltd / WorldAccent

Associate Editor: Nashwa Nasreldin
Series Editor: Erica Hesketh
Cover Design: Kit Humphrey
Printed in the UK by T.J. Books

The author and translator wish to thank the following publications where
previous versions of the English translations were first published:

'Cosmic Haemorrhage': *Another Room to Live In: 15 Contemporary
Arab Poets in Translation* (Litmus Press, 2023) / 'Genetics': *The Arkansas
International* / 'Lot's Wife': *Asymptote* / 'Cigarette of Light', 'My Body,
My Vehicle' and 'The Migrant Poet Slaughters His Voice': *Brooklyn Rail* /
'Perdition' and 'Cities Dying Every Day': *Modern Poetry in Translation* / 'A
Walk', 'In Praise of Modernity': *Paperbag* / 'A Poet': *Poetry London*

The Poetry Translation Centre is supported using public funding
by Arts Council England.

Contents

Introduction

Mona Kareem was born in the Kuwaiti city of Farwaniya in 1987. Her debut poetry collection, *Mornings Washed by Thirst's Water*, was published when she was just 14 years old. 'I was a poet before I was a woman,' Kareem likes to say. Betraying a voracious appetite for engaging with language, she brought us *Absence with Amputated Fingers* two years later. Written in Farwaniya, where she spent the first 23 years of her life, her early work probed weighty themes, among them death, grief and loneliness, in language propelled by surrealism and fragmentation.

The oldest of seven siblings, Kareem shared her father's love of literature, and spent hours helping him to rearrange the books in his prized home library (which he sold during the Gulf War to afford basic necessities, before rebuilding it years later). She was a loving witness to her mother's moments of joy and sadness during that tumultuous period. All the while, Kareem wrote poems in a city where she often felt 'nothing much happened'; where time dragged its feet.

Possibly the most exasperating detail of Kareem's childhood in Kuwait was her status as 'Bidoon'; a stateless Arab minority excluded from receiving citizenship upon the country's independence in 1961. After a period of relatively equal access to public services compared with Kuwaiti nationals, conditions for the Bidoon (short for 'bidoon jinsiya' or 'without nationality') worsened significantly from the 1980s onwards. In fact, just one year before Kareem was born, the Bidoon were categorised as 'illegal residents' and stripped of their access to employment, public education, social welfare and official documentation.

By her early 20s, Kareem's dreams of leaving Kuwait were as old as her body, she recalls. But when she landed in the USA in 2011, on a graduate fellowship to study comparative literature at the State University of New York (SUNY) at Binghamton, she didn't know that the trip would irrevocably alter her reality. The Kuwaiti authorities refused to renew her travel document, shutting her out of the country that housed her family, and thrusting her into a new, precarious status: that of an asylee. That summer marked the second of two chapters of her life. She called it: 'After Exile'.

'Before Exile', Kareem had witnessed the violence of departure and the extended lifespan of mourning within her own household. One of her earliest memories features her mother's family heading to Kuwait's border with Iraq, their belongings wobbling on the roof of the car. At five years old, she couldn't grasp why the women were wailing. It was after the 1990 Gulf War, and local authorities were intensifying their campaign against the Bidoon community, demonising and exiling them en masse, cleaving the Bidoon population in half. Her mother's grief lingered long after her family left, and only deepened with her daughter's departure. After spending a couple of years in New York, Kareem realised that her own separation from her family was, in a way, a continuation of family tradition.

For several years after she arrived in the USA, Kareem recalls feeling stuck in a kind of limbo, a non-place; like the waiting room of an airport or a hospital, where a sense of transience hardens your fingers around your bag – where unpacking seems futile. Reminiscent of the slow rhythm of her life in Farwaniya, exile was also a city where life pulsed much more vibrantly within the confines of her own head.

Her third collection, *What I Sleep for Today*, was published soon after she was granted asylum. While her poetry was garnering international attention and appearing widely in translation (in nine languages so far), she completed a PhD in comparative literature at SUNY. It was also in exile that Kareem made strides in her literary translation career; in English, she published Palestinian poet Ashraf Fayadh's *Instructions Within* in 2016, and a collection of Iraqi poet Ra'ad Abdulqadir's work, *Except for This Unseen Thread*, in 2021. Her trilingual chapbook *Femme Ghosts*, containing Kareem's poems in Arabic along with English and Dutch translations, was published by Publication Studio in 2019.

Kareem currently lives in Boston and is at work on her fourth poetry collection in Arabic, tentatively titled *Words Don't Come Easy*. The past maintains a keen presence in this new book. Alongside poems that pay homage to migrant-artists, including Iraqi authors Sargon Boulous and Saadi Yousef, she also revisits her childhood. She writes about her father's home library, her mother's desperate attempt to save Kareem's eyesight (before succumbing to the inscrutable power of 'genetics'), and about a dream where her mother shows up in New York, with an empty stroller.

Kareem's early poems stand on shaky ground. There is often the sense that the poem doesn't exist behind a closed door; in fact, it doesn't even occupy a self-contained room. At any point, it seems, the poem will abandon its initial direction for the sake of a new one. For instance, in 'A Walk', we are transported significant distances in the span of three brief stanzas. When the poem opens, the speaker's mother is depicted as birthing an extra limb after having her seventh child. The second stanza poignantly captures the river mourning 'the fishermen's departure' (though we don't know why, or where, they have gone). The heartbreaking question that shapes the closure – 'After the government collapses, / who will hand out oxygen masks / to the martyrs?' – suddenly moves us into the realm of political resistance and upheaval.

It is rare for Kareem's work to chart particular places or time periods, a characteristic that often imbues her writing with an apocryphal feeling. In fact, if we were to read her poems as maps, we would be hard pressed to find anything but figurative directions and locations: 'near the ocean's snores'; 'the streets of weariness'; 'the courtyard of my soul'; 'a country where people eat with their eyes'; 'at the fringe of a rock'. Dates and eras are equally obscured; all we get are time conjunctions, or references to day and night – both of which are key characters in Kareem's poetry. Her poems present us with new maps of precarious, unstable and permeable geopolitics. In her essay 'Mapping Exile: A Writer's Story of Growing Up Stateless in Post-Gulf War Kuwait' (*The Common*, 2021), Kareem describes 'rupture' as a facet of the migrant's experience. 'This rupture of time-place-memory-language,' she writes, 'is a shared art among immigrants, who cannot simply carry on across geography.'

If to make a metaphor is to rupture two meanings in favour of a third, then Kareem's poems are relentless rupturers. Relying heavily on metaphors, often to bridge the gap between the self and what lies outside the self, Kareem manipulates language in service of exploring the infinite depths of human experience. The poet is a fish swimming through her lover's ribcage; elsewhere, the poet's body is a car, scratching 'with her unkempt nails / The wooden floors, waiting for language'. (References to language abound across Kareem's oeuvre.) Her poems manifest a porosity between the speaker/poet, nature, and the material world – a porosity that further destabilises the worlds of her poems. 'The bird is a river that sleeps near the Bidoon,' she writes in 'Cosmic Haemorrhage', turning the bird into a river, and then the river into a body in slumber.

Nearly everything seems to have a body in Kareem's poems (even the poem itself). 'The poem lays crucified / over the notepad's knees,' she writes in 'Perdition', a poem constructed of brief, loose fragments. Besides suggesting that both the text and the surface on which the text is inscribed have human bodies, 'Perdition' illustrates the way Kareem uses figurative, surreal language to animate her poems with anthropoid creatures adapted from the natural world; the sky has a breast, the ocean a larynx, and the night a neck, 'strangled / by a choker of stars'.

There is an underlying note of danger in many of Kareem's poems, but the effect is not always perilous – and her tone is remarkably free of pathos; often playful. 'Journey to the

Catacombs of the Heart', for instance, reads as an elegy for a suicidal friend at first glance, before you realise that the protagonist has merely flung herself from the window of the speaker's heart. Kareem also furnishes her poems with characters that seem to herald peril; but their allegorical, almost facetious names – 'Death Policeman', 'Disease Police' – tend to undercut the gravitas of their positions. As a young subversive, Kareem regarded death as the property of adults, and found pleasure in 'trespassing' into this core human experience. She would go on to experiment with the theme of death in various ways – at times for comic relief, at times as a harbinger of new beginnings.

In exile, death has continued to figure in her poems. 'Sometimes I feel like death doesn't belong in the world of exile,' Kareem tells me. 'It's always like a faraway prospect or something that happens in another geography. That's the thing about exile: it deprives you of these basic human tragedies that we all go through.' But as Kareem's first collection in English, *I Will Not Fold These Maps*, shows us, geography is far from a static notion in Kareem's work; she is the author of an impossibly fluid cartography. The impulse in her poems now, after ten years in the USA, is to tempt death, and invite the music of collective mourning that distance mutes. As she writes in 'The Migrant Poet Slaughters His Voice':

> They have stolen our music
> and nothing's left but the voice
>
> that reaches me across time zones
> afflicted with insomnia, burdened with beginnings,
> hanging—like an eternal cry—
> in the chasm of time.

Sara Elkamel

Poems

هلاك

الورودُ تنتحرُ
فوق شرفة سريري
وأمي
تحاولُ دسي في صحراءِ الحياةِ

*

في ساحةِ روحي
شيطانُ صغيرُ
للتو ولد

*

سفينةٌ أخرى
تضيق التنفسَ
على حنجرةِ البحرِ

*

للقمرِ غيمة
في نَهدِ السماءِ

*

الأفكارُ تغرق في التشنجِ
والقصيدةُ
تُصلبُ على ركبتي الكراسة

Perdition

Roses jump to their death
from the rails of my bed
as my mother
tries to tuck me into the desert of life

*

In the courtyard of my soul
is a small devil—
a newborn

*

Another ship
asphyxiates
the ocean's larynx

*

The moon spills a cloud
into the sky's breast

*

Ideas drown in a spasm
and the poem lays crucified
over the notepad's knees

*

الليلُ مختنقٌ
بقلادةِ النجومِ

*

دمعةٌ
تحاولُ الانتحارَ
من هاويةِ عينِي...

*

The night is strangled
by a choker of stars

*

A tear
attempts martyrdom
out of my eye's abyss

بقايا

إنّه الأمس،
حينما تغني شهرزاد
موسيقى الجاز،
و صوتها يحدث خرافة
بين أسِرَّتنا...

أيامها تزامن قيامة أفريقيا،
بينما شوارع الارهاق،
تشعرنا بألف ليلة أخرى
من الدفن

إنّه الأمس إذاً
حيث تهرب الابتسامة
متخفية بين دموع اللاجئين،

نحتاج إلى الموسيقى هنا،
نحتاجها أكثر من شاحنات الخبز

القمر
أفضل الشظايا اِنعزالاً،
والنار تحتضر
قرب شخير البحر

هنالك،
أشلاء من الموت
سكنتني،
كما سكنت الملايين
عند مفرق الغياب

Remains

It is yesterday
when Scheherazade sings jazz,
and her voice forges a myth
in our household.

This coincides with Africa's resurrection,
where the streets of weariness
invoke a thousand more nights
of entombment.

It is yesterday, then,
when the smile escapes,
concealing itself among the tears of refugees.

We need music here.
We need it more than trucks of bread.

The moon
is the most concealed of the shrapnel—
and the fire dwindles
near the ocean's snores.

Fragments of death
have inhabited me,
just as they've inhabited millions
at the junction of absence

وهنالك
ليل يرتدي سترته،
ليأخذ جولة من النحافة
تحوله لهلال معدني

غرفة الاجتماعات مغلقة،
يبدو أنها حفلة خاصة
بالآلهة حيث يحتسون عصير الأرض
تحت أرضية من الحرب

ستبقى لنا الصفعات دائماً
وستبتسم المعرفة
لعقليتي ذات يوم

كنت فضلات الحرب،
لذا استطعت أن أرى الجلاد
وهو يحتضن سوطه
حتى حينما جلدته زوجته

الظلام وسادة النوم،
والرحيل مليء بالعرق
فماذا سنفعل لو استطعنا لصق
السلام في ذهنية الجلادين؟

ماذا،
عن الخريف
الذي سيمزق بدلة الأشجار؟

and night
pulls on his jacket
for an excursion that trims him
into a metallic crescent.

The meeting room is locked;
it seems there's a private party of gods
sipping the juice of the land
beneath the battlefield.

We will always have slaps reserved for us,
and answers will one day
smile at my mind.

I was war's leftovers;
that's how I managed to see the executioner
caressing his whip
even as his wife
whipped him.

Darkness is sleep's pillow,
and departure is drenched in sweat;
what if we could fasten peace
to the psyche of the executioner?

What
of autumn
which will shred the suits of trees?

تمشية

بعد طفلها السابع،
أنجبت أمي قدماً ثالثة.

وفي المدينة
يتسكع النهر طوال الليل،
يبكي فراق الصيادين.

بعد سقوط الحكومة،
من سيوزع أكياس الأكسجين
على الشهداء؟

A Walk

After having her seventh child
my mother gave birth to a third foot.

In the city
the river saunters all night
mourning the fishermen's departure.

After the government collapses,
who will hand out oxygen masks
to the martyrs?

مدن تموت يومياً

عميقة هي الطرقات
بعد أنْ انتهكها الليل
والسكارى...

لن أطوي هذه الخرائط
فهذا سيؤذي أنف وطني
مما يجعله يسلب نقود الشعب
كي يقيم عملية تجميلية

كرة دم أخرى تسير
فوق جسر شرياني النحيف،
فهل ستعترضها شرطة الأمراض؟

الربيع يقع في عقلي الأيسر،
لكن ماذا عن الخريف
طَلَّقَني بعد أن سكن كل حياتي؟

في كل خيمة
هنالك طفل يخرج
من صحراء أمه إلى صحراء أخرى
وأخرى...

تنفس،
دع عملية حفر الرئة علينا،
تنفس،
دع النرجس يغادر روحك

Cities Dying Every Day

The roads are cavernous,
ravaged by night
and the drunkards…

I will not fold these maps;
it might dent my country's nose,
prompting a raid on all our pockets
for emergency plastic surgery.

Another blood cell treads
along my artery's narrow bridge—
will the Disease Police intercept it?

Spring lies in my left brain,
but what of autumn?
Is it possible it has divorced me,
after inhabiting my entire life?

Inside every tent
is a child who emerges
out of its mother's desert and into another desert
and then another…

Breathe,
leave the task of lung excavation to us.
Breathe,
let Narcissus depart your soul.

أطنان من الغبار
تغطي عروقنا
لكنها ليست كما الغبار
الذي يغطي ابتساماتنا

كثير من المدن تموت يومياً،
وأنا مت حينما قرر سومر
التنازل عن عرشه

آسيا
للمرة المليون تلبس معطفاً
من الحروب،
بينما أعمارنا تتحول
لقطارات هرمة..

Tonnes of dust
shroud our veins,
but it cannot compare to the dust
that shrouds our smiles.

Many cities die every day;
I myself died
when Sumer decided
to surrender the throne.

For the millionth time, Asia
dons a coat of wars—
as our lives transform
into aging trains.

الطريق إلى مقبرة القلب

نسيت أن أضع سلماً للطوارئ،
نسيت أن أبني قلبي بشكل منخفض،
صديقة أخرى تنتحر من نافذة قلبي.
هل لي أن أتشبث بحجابها الأبيض لأنقذها؟

لربما نصف صديقة، وجه يحبني، وآخر متجهم.
أعلم: كانت تغسل ثيابها يومياً من نكاتي السخيفة.

أعلم أيضاً: جنود صغار حولوا وسادتها لساحة معركة،
جعلوني قائداً عسكرياً يقصف أحلامها.

من سيحدثني الآن يا صديقتي عن عاشق وهمي؟

سأترك الأكواب فارغة
فحتى الشاي يا صديقتي
لن يوقظكِ من موتك.

Journey to the Catacombs of the Heart

I forgot to install an emergency staircase.
I forgot to construct my heart closer to the ground;
another friend has flung herself from the window of my heart.
Can I still grab hold of her white veil; can I save her?

Perhaps she was only half a friend;
one countenance loving, the other sullen.
I know she cleansed her clothes, daily, of my silly jokes.

I also know how tiny soldiers converted her pillow
into a battlefield;
I was cast as a military commander, shelling her dreams.

Who will talk to me now
of make-believe lovers?

I will leave the cups empty.
For even tea, my friend,
will not rouse you from your death.

سيجارة ضوء

ما الذي أنام من أجله اليوم؟
أحلم أن أفتحَ قفصَه الصدري
وأسبح فيه كسمكةٍ تجفف دموعها.

يقول:
ألم تعرفي أن الحمامات الإلكترونية
هزمت الحمامات الطيبة؟!

توجد في روحي
زفرات كبيرة،
خلقها أطفال لا ينامون.

يوجد في روحي
مقبض مكسور.

الظلام:
أن تضع الضوء في جيبك
وترحل.

Cigarette of Light

What do I sleep for today?
I part his ribcage open in my dream;
I swim through it like a fish
drying its tears.

He says:
Didn't you hear that electronic pigeons
have overthrown the good old pigeons?!

Lodged in my soul are the thunderous sighs
of insomniac children.

Lodged in my soul
is a broken doorknob.

Darkness
is to slip the light into your pocket,
and be on your way.

نزيف الكونية

١
المطر اندماج مشترك

٢
الليل يقف خجولاً في قلبي

٣
نهر يغرق،
هل ينتحب مثلي؟

٤
تلتقطني بحياء،
أطالعها:
روحها في يدي،
وكلماتها تهطل فيّ

٥
ثقب من الأبديّة
لا تمنحه غير الأمهات

٦
يغسل روحه بالمُطهر،
أملاً في الهرب من الفلسفة

٧
الخطيئة تختبئ تحت قميصي

Cosmic Haemorrhage

1
Rain is an affair of fusion

2
Night lingers timidly in my heart

3
A river drowns in itself
Does it weep like I do?

4
She picks me up timidly,
I pore over her:
Her soul is in my hands,
Her words pour down inside me

5
A cavity of eternity
That only mothers can give

6
He disinfects his soul,
Hoping to escape philosophy

7
Sin conceals itself below my shirt

٨

ألتقط ما تبقى من دموع جدتي،
فهي المفتاح الوحيد لنحيينا

٩

البكاء يخرج من بيتي،
آه،
كم أنا مشتاقة للغطس فيه

١٠

أتصفح روحي:
لا شيء غير اللعنة

١١

ملابسي تملأ فضاء المدنس،
وخصوصيتي تداعب السماء

١٢

معلقون في الطهارة،
نحاول اجتذاب أطراف الابتسامة

١٣

الناي عين الأرض

١٤

الحقيقة تتعرى،
علها تقتل الأشجار

8

I catch what's left of my grandmother's tears,
The only keys to our grief

9

Weeping vacates my house;
O!
How I miss diving in it

10

I flip through the pages of my soul:
I find nothing but damnation

11

My outfit permeates an irreverent cosmos
And my privacy teases the sky

12

Suspended in purity,
We try to draw the edges of a smile

13

The flute is the eye of the earth

14

The truth strips naked,
Perhaps it could murder the trees

١٥
أعلق بكائي على الباب،
ريثما ألتقيه في المطهر

١٦
أيقونة الغربة =
قميص ووجه من الحزن
يتصفح الأحذية ليلاً

١٧
الوطن يستحم بدماء الفقراء

١٨
أصنع طيراً يتذكر أحضان جدتي

١٩
أمي تختبئ في علبة كبريت،
أبي يشعلها

٢٠
قصيدة أخرى تقع من ذاكرتي

٢١
البنات يعانقن الحقيقة،
كم هن غبيات في حبهن لهذا الحيوان

٢٢
الذاكرة تتألم حينما تسمع إمرأة
ترقص بلا رحمة

15
I hang my tears on the door,
Until we meet in purgatory

16
The stamp of estrangement:
A shirt and a face cloaked in gloom
Browsing shoes in the night

17
The nation bathes in the blood of the poor

18
I build a bird who recalls my grandmother's embrace

19
My mother hides in a matchbox;
My father ignites her

20
Yet another poem plummets from my memory

21
Girls embrace the truth
How foolish of them to love this animal

22
Memory aches at the sound of a woman
Dancing without mercy

23
We enter adolescence:
A demon, and a worker
Trampling us with socialism

24
Lethargy grows long fingers in the night

25
Life begins to wail
The moment my senses fail me

26
Birds persecute my thoughts

27
A hammer, a nail, and other tools
To hang light near the window

28
The earth veils itself with rain

29
Winter enfolds the truth
Whenever shadows wander

30
Nietzsche is quite handsome
Despite his philosophical fractures

31
Darkness lingers lonely in this school

32
Despair longs to embrace the flute

33
Light departs this contrarian horizon

34
Wounds nick Salvador Dali's painting;
Ridicule circles Frida Kahlo's body

35
Only a fool stares into the face of a woman;
It would be in his best interest to replace her
With a more favourable god

36
The bird is a river that sleeps near the Bidoon

37
Sin only sleeps near women

38
The moon implores me to dig a grave of death

39
Your voice sets off a dance in my lungs

٤٠

الوطن يلد ظلماً مستأجراً

٤١

لحن من التحيات يراني تمثالاً مؤلماً

٤٢

التصوف يلطخ سمعة الفساد

٤٣

نساء سورياليات
يحلقن في رأسي،
ترى هل سيرسمن نميمة مفتوحة؟!

٤٤

خراف تتعرى من القتل،
و العدم يشبهها ببنت الجيران

٤٥

الحياة تعيش غيبوبة من الحروب

٤٦

البياض في يدي
النزيف للكونية...

40

The nation gives birth to a leased injustice

41

A melody of greetings finds me
A throbbing statue

42

Sufism tarnishes the name of corruption

43

Surreal women
Flutter around my head;
I wonder if they'll paint open-ended gossip!

44

Sheep are murdered and stripped;
Their nothingness mirrors the neighbour's daughter

45

Life resides in a coma of wars

46

Whiteness is in my hands
A haemorrhage for the cosmos…

جسدي مركبتي

جسدي مركبتي
أقودها مثل مراهق مستهتر
تصطدم بالآخرين، بالأرصفة
تجتاز الإشارة الحمراء في الثانية الأخيرة
فيهز شرطي الموت رأسه

أحيانا أفقد ملامحاً أو خصلةً أو عضواً
ولا أجد قطع غيار في السكراب
خسرت شفاهي الفضية
وقلبي المغطى بالشحوم
وخسرت قبعتي المتحركة
ثم يدي اليسرى
التي أرى من خلالها الآخرين

مثل رجل كندي في أيام الاثنين
أشغلها بهدوء وأجرف الثلج من حولها
أدعها تسخن وتصحصح
تستعيد حواسها
فلا مركبة تنهض من السرير
مستعدة لمواجهة الشارع

في الغرفة أدعها تحوم
كلما اختنقت الفكرة
تخدش أظافرها المهملة
خشب الأرض بانتظار اللغة
تخرج والغصة تزول

My Body, My Vehicle

My body is my vehicle
I drive her like a reckless teen
She crashes into others, into sidewalks
She breaks red lights at the last second
As the Death Policeman shakes his head

Sometimes, I lose one of my features, a strand of hair,
or an organ
And I find no spare parts in the junkyard
I lose my silver lips
And my grease-coated heart
I lose my rotating hat
Then, my left hand
And with it, my peripheral vision

Like a Canadian on Mondays
I start the engine softly and shovel the surrounding snow
I let her warm up and come alive
Regain her senses
For no vehicle rises from bed
Ready to face the street

In the room, I let her roam
Every time an idea struggles for air
She scratches with her unkempt nails
The wooden floors, waiting for language
Until it unfurls, easing the crisis

ما الذي عليّ فعله بمركبتي هذي؟
لا يمكنني ركنها وهجرها في أي مكان!
حين أذهب للتسوق تحطم عجلاتي
السيراميك اللامع
وحين أنزل إلى البحر
تنغرس في الرمال

صغيرة وسمراء ومحطمة
زجاجها سجل الريح
وصوتها يتداعى في ساعة الزحام

What do I do with this vehicle of mine?
I cannot park her, abandon her anywhere!
When I go shopping, my wheels shatter
The glossy ceramic floors
And when I go to the beach
She sinks into the sand

Small and dark, complected and broken
Her windows are an almanac of winds
And her voice falters at rush hour

في فوائد الحداثة

قد أكون سلحفاة،
تقودني بحقيبتك
بينما يغزو دخانك نصف المدينة.

وحدها السلحفاة قادرة على رؤية كل شيء:
الفتاة التي ارتدت حجاباً
لأنها تعبت من تسريح شعرها،
الشاب الذي يجمع الفقه بالهب هوب،
والدولة العميقة التي نستمني في حفرها.

أمي تعّرف غربتي بفقدان رائحتي التي تتوهمها،
أنا أعرّف غربتي في علاقتي مع غسالة الملابس..

وحدها المغاسل العامة في أمريكا
تحترم التعددية الثقافية،
فقد تغسل ملابسك بعد عدوك
واهماً بأن العرق لن يختلط!

أنا أحب المدينة،
وأحب الحداثة فعلاً،
فقط لأنني لا أطيق الحشرات!

In Praise of Modernity

I could be a turtle
you drive around in your bag,
while your fumes invade half the city.

Only the turtle can witness it all:
The girl who started wearing hijab
having given up on styling her hair,
the young man who fuses Hip Hop with Fiqh,
and the Deep State, in whose pits we masturbate.

My mother defines my expatriation
by the desiccation of the smell she loves;
I define my expatriation
by my relationship to the washing machine.

Only laundromats in America
respect cultural diversity—
you might wash your clothes after your enemy's,
convinced that your sweat
won't mingle!

I love the city.
And I really do love modernity—
if only because I can't stand insects!

جينات

لا يمكنك الوثوق بشخص لا يحب البرتقال

كان لي مرة صديقة تكره البرتقال
تعصر عينيها جزءاً من رائحته
تقول إنها تفضل العطور
أو حتى رائحة رز محترق

شفاهها المكتنزة لا تحمل أي مشاعر
تجاه العصائر بمرارتها وحلاوتها أو دبقها
حتى أن أسنانها لم تألف عملية تعرية البرتقالة
أو تعرية أي جلد على العموم

أنا أيضاً كان لي ثمرة كرهتها
في تلك الأيام السحيقة
عندما كنا نجلس على أرض الله
النساء في وضعية بوذا والرجال متقرفصين
نحاصر رأس معزة
تقف فوق جبل من الرز
كشمعة ميلاد

نجتمع في دائرة كحشد فاتته أفعال المقصلة
لكنه قد يشهد لفظة الروح. كنت أحبذ الرأس
– ذاك الملك المغدور محشواً بالشموخ –
بأصابعي الطويلة أجره نحو حدودي
بينما أفرز البصلات الصغيرة بعيداً عنه

ولدت في بلد يأكل فيها الناس بأعينهم
وبإمكانهم حتى استقدام عمالة تأكل بالنيابة عنهم
فيحافظوا على أسنانهم لارتكاب خطايا أكبر

Genetics

You can't trust someone who doesn't like oranges.

I once had a friend who hated oranges—
she'd squeeze her eyes shut, repulsed by the scent.
She said she preferred perfume,
or even the smell of burnt rice.

Her plump lips held no emotion
towards the bitterness, sweetness, or stickiness of juice—
her teeth were strangers to the stripping of an orange
and the stripping of skin in general.

I too had a fruit I hated
in those abysmal days,
when we would sit on God's soil,
the women in Buddha pose, the men squatting
around the head of a goat
that stood on a mountain of rice
like a birthday candle.

We gathered in a circle,
like a crowd that had arrived too late to the guillotining,
but in time to witness the final utterance
of the soul. I loved the head
—the betrayed king, stuffed with pride—
my long fingers dragged him towards my edges,
flinging small onions to the side.

I was born to a country where people eat with their eyes—
they can even hire workers to eat on their behalf,

يتشاكى بعضهم: كيف تكون الطماطم حمراء هكذا
وبلا سكر

ثم في يوم قرر أبي شراء طاولة طعام:
لم يعد لأصابعنا أماكن تغوص فيها وتحفر
ولا دروب تلاحق عبرها حلقات البصل
مستوين على الكراسي جلس الرجال والنساء
بينما ظلت صحيفة اليوم جائعة على الكنبة.
اليوم أقضم البصلة كما لو أنها تفاحة

أو جزراً كانت تعصره أمي
أملاً بإنقاذ عينّي
في مهمة مثلت الامتحان الأول لأمومتها

سألت أمي الطبيب "هل صحيح أن الجزر يساعد؟"
فهز رأسه إيجاباً لأن في ذهنه الفلاح ذكره سؤالها
بنكتة عن كون الأطفال حميراً والأمهات ساحرات

كل يوم راحت تعصر الجزر
حتى بات كل شيء بطعم الجزر
وتفتحت عيناي إلى رؤى وكوابيس وقصص
عن أم قلبت ابنتها حماراً

من وقتها لم تحاول أمي انقاذي ثانية
"لا شيء ينفع" تقول،
لم تعد تؤمن بالخضراوات والفواكه
ولا الأمومة والتطبيب.
"لا يمكن علاج الأفواه والعيون" تقول،
"لا يمكن هزيمة الجينات."

to save their own teeth for greater sins.
Some of them complain: How can tomatoes be so red,
and so sugarless?

Then one day, my father decided to buy a dining table.
Suddenly, there was nowhere for our fingers to dive
and dig; no pathways lined with onion rings.
Men and women sat equal on chairs
as today's newspaper lingered hungry on the sofa.
Today, I bite into onions like apples,

or the carrots my mother would juice
desperate to save my eyesight
on the mission that shaped the first test of her motherhood.

'Is it true carrots can help?' my mother asked the doctor,
who nodded with a grin, for in his peasant-brain
her question recalled a hilarious fable
where children are donkeys, and mothers witches.

Every day she squeezed carrots
until everything tasted like carrots
and my eyes opened to visions, nightmares, and stories
of a woman who turned her daughter into a donkey.

That was the last time my mother tried to save me.
'There's no point,' she said.
She no longer believed in fruits and vegetables,
or motherhood, or medicine.
'You cannot cure mouths or eyes,' she said.
'You cannot compete with genetics.'

شاعرة

إلى إيتل عدنان

كتبت قصيدةً عن حبها
و تركتها في الشرفةِ،
أتى حبيبها وسرقها

لأنها منعزلة جداً
تحاول دائماً أن تكتبَ
عن أصدقاء متخيلين
يطلبون منها قصيدة
مقابل دعوتها للعشاء

نزعت أحلامها فوق الورقة
واحدة تلو الأخرى
ثم ذهبت لتنتحر

مرةً أهملت كل أحبتها
في جوفِ الكراسةِ
فماتوا برصاصات طائشة.

A Poet

for Etel Adnan

She wrote a love poem
and left it on the balcony—
her lover appeared
and swiped it.

Because of her extreme isolation,
she wrote constantly
of imaginary friends
who pressed her for poems
in exchange for dinner invitations.

She expelled her dreams, one at a time,
onto sheets of paper—
before she fled
to take her own life.

One time, she abandoned all her lovers
in her notebook's caverns—
they died in a massacre
of stray bullets.

والهة

عند المدخل، وقفت امرأة لوط وقد سخطها الفنان إلى شكل أقسى مما فعل الرب. لم يحافظ على جسدها الملحي، بل رممها بالبرونز لتظل حبيسة الأزلية. ليس بإمكانها زيارة جيرانها لتخبرهم عن زوارها الجدد، حتى عتبة الغاليري لا يمكنها تجاوزها. ساكنة محنطة، تسمع الحوارات العابرة وترصد الوجوه بعينين فارغتين من التشويق. تمر من أمامها أجناس شتى كل يوم: جن وإنس وملائكة وأنبياء. كانت في حياة سابقة تتلوّى إن اضطرت للحفاظ على حكايا الغرباء في بطنها، تدور في الحي تستفرغها واحدة تلو الأخرى.

الآن لم تعد تشكل خطراً على الأسرار. الآن، تدفع والهة ثمن حنينها السريع، ثمن شغفها بالماضي، الذي اضطرها لإلقاء نظرة أخيرة على سدوم. في نظرة، بالكاد سجلت ألوان حياتها، بالكاد حبست رائحة الصباح قبل أن تضيع مع الجغرافيا، بالكاد ابتلعت لغة ستنتهي أحلامها بانتفائها. في النقطة الحدودية، ليس مسموح للمهاجر أن يشغل نفسه بأي شيء سوى اللحظة الراهنة. قالوا إنها بالتفاتتها فضحت هوية الرب. أو أنها في أعماقها آمنت بأن سدوم بريئة، بأن سدوم لا تستحق أن تدك هكذا حتى الرماد.

ربما لو انتظرت والهة حتى وصلت إلى الكهف قبل أن تترك للحنين أن يغمرها، لذهبت قصة الكونية في اتجاه آخر تماماً. بل لربما انتهت في ذاك الكهف واسترحنا. لما لم يتفهم الرب أنها أرادت فقط ما يكفي لكتابة قصيدة أطلال؟ هل لأن الطلل حصر على الرجال؟

صغيرة تبدو فوق المكعب، رأسها كما جنين لا موهبة له في الصراخ. جردها الفنان من ذراعيها ورجليها. لربما خاف الفنان أن تهرب امرأة لوط من الغاليري وتعود مرة أخرى إلى العالم السفلي.

Lot's Wife

Lot's wife stands near the entrance, deformed more radically by the artist than she had ever been by the Lord. The artist didn't preserve her salty body; instead, he recast her in bronze, crafting a prisoner of eternity. She can't visit the neighbours to gossip about her new patrons; she can't even cross the gallery's threshold. Mummified and silent, she overhears fleeting conversations, surveils countenances with incurious eyes. Jinn, humans, angels and prophets walk past her daily. In a previous life, she squirmed when she had to carry strangers' stories in her belly—so she wandered the neighbourhood, disgorging one tale after the other.

She is no longer a threat to secrets. Now, Lot's wife pays the price for her fleeting nostalgia, her passion for the past, which compelled her to take one last look at Sodom. Looking back, she barely managed to archive the colours of her life, barely captured the morning's scent before it went missing, together with geography. She barely swallowed the language whose extinction would render her dreams obsolete. At the border checkpoint, a migrant is not allowed to occupy herself with anything but the present moment. They said that in turning back, she had compromised the identity of the Lord. Or that in her gut, she believed Sodom innocent, wrongly battered to dust.

Perhaps if she had waited until she reached the cave before letting nostalgia overwhelm her, the plot of cosmology would have gone in an entirely different direction. In fact, it might have ended in that cave, and left us in peace. Why wouldn't the Lord understand that all she wanted was to write a poem about ruins? Is it because men have a sole claim to ruin?

She looks tiny on the plinth; her head like a newborn with no talent for wailing. The artist has stripped Lot's wife of her limbs. Perhaps he feared she would escape the gallery, and travel back to the underworld.

الشاعر المهجري يذبح صوته

في صيف حارق
- أحرق من الصيف الماضي،
وأبرد من التالي –
نزل الشاعر من الجنوب الأعلى
إلى الجنوب الأدنى

نزل ثم وقف على حافة الصخرة
وذبح صوته. هكذا بكل هدوء،
رمشت عيناه الضيقتان بانزعاج.
لم يقرأ الفاتحة ولم يحدد لله
لمن يهدي هذا القربان.

لقد زهق الشاعر من كون صوته استعارة،
أراد أن يرى دم صوته، شحمه ولحمه،
حسبه ونسبه، أن يسمع اهتزاز الحبال
حتى لو تكلفه لفظة الموت.

في لغتنا، يجد نفسه مقدماً الاسم على الفعل،
لوثة الأنا الغنائية ربما. يقطف كلمات
تيبست حتى استحالت ذهباً، ينفض عنها
غبار القرون ثم يغرسها في أصص صغيرة.
يظن الشاعر أن بإمكانه
ابراء الأكم واحياء الموتى.

أما في لغتهم، يقطع الجبال والمحيطات
تاركاً طلاسم على كل شجرة
كي لا يستحيل إلى مرايا.

The Migrant Poet Slaughters His Voice

One scorching summer
—hotter than the previous summer,
and cooler than the next—
the poet journeyed from the upper south
to the lower south.

He descended, and at the fringe of a rock,
slaughtered his voice. Just like that, calmly,
his narrow eyes squinting in distress.
He did not read Al-Fatiha, nor did he pledge
this sacrifice to Allah.

The poet was exasperated that his voice had become
a metaphor; he wanted to see the blood
of his voice, its grease and flesh,
its lineage—to hear its chords vibrating
even if a single utterance would cost him his life.

In our language, he finds himself placing nouns before verbs,
tainted by the lyrical I, perhaps. He picks words
that had wilted until they turned to gold. Wiping away
the dust of centuries, he plants them in small pots.
The poet thinks he can
heal the dumb, and revive the dead.

Meanwhile, in their language,
he crosses mountains and oceans,
leaving a talisman on every tree
to escape entrapment in mirrors.

يأتي بجبل من سفوح كاليفورنيا
ثم يلقي به في خليج المكسيك
ليطفو ثانية فوق أنبوب نفط.

كل صباح، أستيقظ على صوته،
أوصد الشباك في وجهه لأكمل نومي.
أتركه يلخبط الساعات، يحدثني عن قصيدة النثر
كيف تقف كجذع أجرد قاطعة الأفق:
لقد سرقوا موسيقانا
ولم يتبق سوى الصوت

يصلني مع فارق التوقيت
مريضاً بالأرق، مثقلاً بالبدايات،
عالقاً – كصرخة أزلية –
في هوة الوقت.

He hauls a mountain from the slopes of California,
and flings it into the Gulf of Mexico
before it floats, once again, atop an oil pipeline.

Every morning I wake up to his voice;
I slam the window shut, and go back to sleep.
I let him jumble the clocks, talk to me
about the prose poem—
how it stands like a bare trunk, interrupting the horizon:
They have stolen our music
and nothing's left but the voice

that reaches me across time zones
afflicted with insomnia, burdened with beginnings,
hanging—like an eternal cry—
in the chasm of time.

Afterword

Mona Kareem cannot go home again. That much became clear when, on the 3rd of January 2023, she boarded a flight in Beirut, hoping to reunite with her family in Kuwait after years of separation. Instead, she was immediately detained on arrival at Kuwait International Airport and subjected to lengthy interrogations. If Kareem insisted on trying to enter the country, the authorities told her, she would be thrown into prison. In their eyes, she had committed an unforgivable sin: she had chosen to publicly criticize the Kuwaiti government's mistreatment of her people. The authorities didn't even bother to veil their threats. After all, why would they, given that Kuwait is an absolute monarchy where disenfranchised expatriates account for 60 per cent of the total population, and where the stateless Bidoon, the Arab minority from which Kareem hails, have become an exploited and maligned underclass. Thus, Kareem took the only option left to her and she was deported back to the USA, where she has lived for over a decade, and where she has since acquired citizenship. Her dreams of return dashed, she resumed her life in exile.

I had the distinct pleasure of publishing Kareem's epic chronicle of her life in the USA, 'Dying Like A Statue', in the Spring 2022 issue of *Poetry London*. In this poem we find Kareem earning minimum wage at a university in New York, teaching students 'about women / in arranged marriages', or sitting on an airplane 'surrounded / by black soldiers, sleeping and dreaming / of Iraqis they had to kill // In 16 hours, you lost your country / for the second time, a country / no one can love'. Kareem is right: it's hard to love the Gulf, especially if you have spent your life watching governments denying you access to citizenship, public services, employment and travel. However, the reception Kareem receives on the other side, in her new home, isn't exactly warm, either: 'Behind the bullet-proof glass, the visa officer smiles down at me like a drone. She is happy with my bare head, with my good English, with my assurances that I do not intend to remain in the United States, who are we kidding? *Literature?* she repeats after me, *what is there to write about the desert?* I sweat staring at her little camera, offering my fingers, DNA, face and eyes, a generous gift to the national archive.'

The ostracisation endured by Kareem over the course of her life has made her a fully-fledged member of that denationalised tribe that encompasses all kinds of expatriates, stateless and the politically disenfranchised, the amorphous community that makes up anywhere between 50 and 90 per cent of the populations of all Gulf countries. Kareem reflected on this in her essay 'Bidoon: A Cause and Its Literature Are Born': 'In exile, I have met other Gulf peoples. Their origins on paper are India, or Iran, or Egypt, or the Philippines, and some of them write in English, but they were born and raised in the Gulf and then ended up in exile for one reason or another.' Indeed, exile is the only destination that was ever on the cards for people like us. After all, we of the Gulf are defined by what we are not: citizens. We have little in common with those whom Hannah Arendt called the *Heimatlosen* – the stateless ones, namely nations of peoples without a state, for example the Palestinians and the Kurds, peoples who ultimately aspire to found a nation-state, or rather, re-found one. One might even say that we have more in common with Salman Rushdie's Midnight Children's Conference than with the registered inhabitants of sovereign states. Indeed, we are a new Lost Tribe, relying on the mercy of short-term contracts, long-term visas and sanctuary cities, traveling the world in search of work: one world cup stadium here, a power-plant there, contributing to economies across six continents, none of which will ever have to look after us in return. The novelist Deepak Unnikrishnan, one of our brightest voices, has called us temporary people. You could also call us disposable transients. Not that we aren't critically important to the global economy. Just as capital needs to circulate to feed the murderous cycle of our economies, so must the people that fulfill all the lowest jobs in those economies, for theirs is the blood that greases this planetary machine. Surely, as our world integrates further, this amorphous community of migrant workers, who can hold no state, or corporation accountable, is only set to increase. The victims of natural disasters, financial downturns, violence and war will swell their numbers, and they will have no parliaments to represent them, no embassies to turn to, and no passports to bring them 'home'.

This is why Kareem's work isn't available for sale in Kuwait, even though she's a rising star in the English-speaking world and has been translated into nine languages. Her absence from bookshelves yields unfortunate proof of how the Gulf petrocracies have attempted to eradicate all freethinking from their societies. The irony is that while Islamophobic books written by white orientalists and published by western presses may be purchased in any Gulf bookshops, you won't find Abdelrahman Munif's *Cities of Salt*, or Kareem's work, or mine, because they've all been banned, in one way or another. This is the heart of the loneliness present in these poems, where Kareem describes her peripatetic life with painful poignancy, 'I was born to a country where people eat with their eyes— / they can even hire workers to eat on their behalf, / to save their own teeth for greater sins' she tells us in 'Genetics', one of the collection's standout poems.

The implied resistance of the collection's title, *I Will Not Fold These Maps*, neatly encapsulates the author's refusal to be circumscribed by borders and nations. In her poems, artfully translated by the Egyptian poet and journalist Sara Elkamel, Kareem is a stranger who is always on the verge of coming and going, leaving a dust cloud in her wake as she travels through nameless cities, so much so that in her poem 'My Body, My Vehicle', she writes:

My body is my vehicle
I drive her like a reckless teen
She crashes into others, into sidewalks
She breaks red lights at the last second
As the Death Policeman shakes his head

Kareem's natural habitat, especially in the more recent poems drawn from *Words Don't Come Easy*, is now the desert of exile. Yet there is nothing dead, or sterile, or inhuman about this desert. It is only in exile that a writer may hit upon the naked realities all too often concealed by the bubble of the nation-state, and in Kareem's poems, out of the desert emerges the vision of the poem as an oasis, allowing the poem itself to become the only place worth returning to, a fixed point on the horizon. Her critical gaze is unforgiving, yet always lyrical, and although her surreal turns are delightful, they never get in the way of her ability to both remain rooted in the moment and cast an eye towards history, tracing the genealogy of our rootless discontent from our earliest beginnings. As a case in point, I offer up these lines from one of my favourite poems of hers, 'Lot's Wife', a dramatisation of the moment when the eponymous heroine is turned into a pillar of salt when she turns to take one last look at Sodom: 'Looking back, she barely managed to archive the colours of her life, barely captured the morning's scent before it went missing, together with geography. She barely swallowed the language whose extinction would render her dreams obsolete. At the border checkpoint, a migrant is not allowed to occupy herself with anything but the present moment. They said that in turning back, she had compromised the identity of the Lord. Or that in her gut, she believed Sodom innocent, wrongly battered to dust.'

André Naffis-Sahely

Mona Kareem is the author of three poetry collections. Her poetry has been translated into nine languages, and appeared (in English) in: *POETRY, Poetry Northwest, Michigan Quarterly, Poetry London* and *Modern Poetry in Translation*, among others. She is a recipient of a 2021 literary grant from the National Endowment for the Arts. Kareem holds a PhD in Comparative Literature and works as an assistant professor of Middle East Studies at Washington University St. Louis. Her translations include Ashraf Fayadh's *Instructions Within* (nominated for a BTBA award), Ra'ad Abdulqadir's *Except for this Unseen Thread*, and Octavia Butler's *Kindred*.

Photo courtesy of Sima Diab

Sara Elkamel is a poet, journalist and literary translator. Her debut chapbook, *Field of No Justice*, was published by the African Poetry Book Fund & Akashic Books in 2021, and her poems have appeared in international literary journals and anthologies. She holds an MA in arts journalism from Columbia University and an MFA in poetry from New York University.

André Naffis-Sahely is the author of two collections of poetry, *The Promised Land: Poems from Itinerant Life* (Penguin UK, 2017) and *High Desert* (Bloodaxe Books, 2022), as well as the editor of *The Heart of a Stranger: An Anthology of Exile Literature* (Pushkin Press, 2020). He has translated over twenty titles of fiction, poetry and nonfiction, including works by Honoré de Balzac, Émile Zola, Abdellatif Laâbi, Ribka Sibhatu and Tahar Ben Jelloun. His writing appears regularly in the pages of the *Times Literary Supplement*, *The Baffler* and *Poetry* (Chicago), among others. He is a Lecturer at the University of California, Davis in the USA and the editor of *Poetry London* in the UK.

About the Poetry Translation Centre

Set up in 2004, the Poetry Translation Centre is the only UK organisation dedicated to translating, publishing and promoting contemporary poetry from Africa, Asia, the Middle East and Latin America. We introduce extraordinary poets from around the world to new audiences through books, online resources and bilingual events. We champion diversity and representation in the arts and forge enduring relations with diaspora communities in the UK. We explore the craft of translation through our long-running programme of workshops which are open to all.

The Poetry Translation Centre is based in London and is an Arts Council National Portfolio organisation. To find out more about us, including how you can support our work, please visit: www.poetrytranslation.org.

About the World Poet Series

The *World Poet Series* offers an introduction to some of the world's most exciting contemporary poets in an elegant pocket-sized format. The books are presented as dual-language editions, with the English and original-language text displayed side by side. They include specially commissioned translations and completing each book is an afterword essay by an English-language poet, responding to the translations.